LIFE SCIENCES CONTRIBUTION
ROYAL ONTARIO MUSEUM
NUMBER 126

CW00518147

QMC   3U2UU5 ʳ

a30213 003020057b

ED LANDING
ROLF LUDVIGSEN
PETER H. von BITTER

Upper Cambrian to Lower Ordovician Conodont Biostratigraphy and Biofacies, Rabbitkettle Formation, District of Mackenzie

RŎM

Canadian Cataloguing in Publication Data

Landing, Ed.
   Upper Cambrian to Lower Ordovician conodont biostratigraphy and biofacies, Rabbit-kettle Formation, District of Mackenzie

(Life sciences contributions; no. 126 ISSN 0384-8159) Bibliography: p.

ISBN 0-88854-265-8 pa.

1. Conodonts. 2. Paleontology—Cambrian. 3. Paleontology—Ordovician. 4. Paleontology—Northwest Territories—Mackenzie. I. Ludvigsen, Rolf, 1944-   II. Von Bitter, Peter H., 1942-   III. Royal Ontario Museum. IV. Title V. Series.

QE899.L36   562'.2'097193   C80-094632-4

Publication date: 10 October 1980
ISBN 0-88854-265-8
ISSN 0384-8159

Upper Cambrian to Lower Ordovician Conodont Biostratigraphy and Biofacies, Rabbitkettle Formation, District of Mackenzie

Abstract

Conodonts have been recovered from two sections through the Cambrian-Ordovician boundary beds of the upper Rabbitkettle Formation, near the headwaters of the Broken Skull River, western Mackenzie Mountains. The two sections are separated by a thrust fault. The sequence of trilobite faunas from the low-energy outer shelf facies of the Rabbitkettle is equivalent to the *Saukiella junia* through *Symphysurina brevispicata* subzones from the inner carbonate platform in Oklahoma and Texas. Significant differences in trilobite faunas between the Mackenzie Mountains and United States sequences represent contrasting biofacies developments. Similarly, the sparse and low diversity conodont faunas of the Rabbitkettle resemble coeval Appalachian continental slope and outer shelf faunas rather than those reported from the inner carbonate platform in Texas and Utah. The *Proconodontus* and *Cordylodus oklahomensis* (new name) zones can be recognized in the Rabbitkettle but cannot be divided into the subzones established in Utah. These data suggest that lithofacies associations and biofacies developments in conodont distribution may prohibit detailed conodont-based correlations of Cambrian-Ordovician boundary beds.

Introduction

Uppermost Cambrian and lowest Ordovician conodonts are known from sections in the western United States (Miller, 1969, 1970, 1975, 1977, 1978; Kurtz, 1976), Alberta (Derby et al., 1972), Iran (Müller, 1973), and Australia (Druce and Jones, 1971). The similarities of conodont faunal sequences in these widely separated areas have been interpreted to reflect a lack of or weak development of conodont biofacies or provincialism in Cambrian-Ordovician boundary beds (Barnes et al., 1973). Land-

1

ing et al. (1978) suggested that conodont faunas bridge the biofacies differences shown by trilobites. Consequently, conodonts have received considerable discussion in intercontinental correlation of Cambrian-Ordovician boundary beds (Jones et al., 1971; Miller, 1977, 1978; Landing et al., 1978).

Available lithologic information indicates that the North American, Iranian, and Australian conodont successions listed above were derived from intertidal or very shallow sublittoral, inner carbonate platform sequences. Similarities of the faunal successions may reflect the appearance of comparable conodont assemblages (''communities'') in similar but geographically separated environments.

Based on studies of continental slope deposits in the northern Appalachians, Landing (1978, 1979) proposed that major conodont biofacies differences existed during the uppermost Cambrian and lowest Ordovician. Faunas from inner carbonate platform sequences appear to differ from those in sequences deposited in environments with unrestricted access to the open ocean.

The upper Rabbitkettle Formation in the western Mackenzie Mountains (Fig. 1) has lithologic and faunal features representative of an open shelf facies. The trilobite

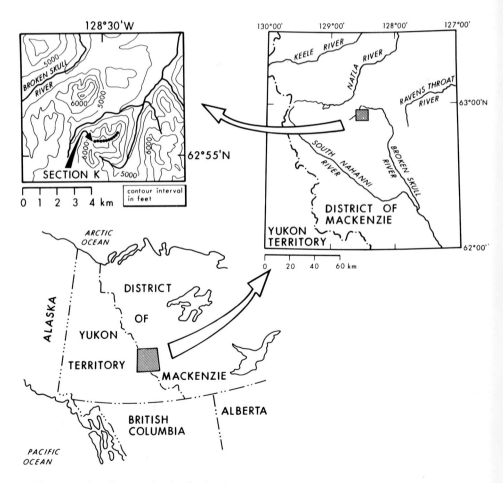

Fig. 1   Locality maps showing Section K.

2

sequence from this interval, briefly summarized in this report, can be correlated with those from the uppermost Cambrian to lowest Ordovician successions of Texas (Winston and Nicholls, 1967; Longacre, 1970) and Oklahoma (Stitt, 1971, 1977) although significant differences in faunal composition are present. These differences are attributed to the more open marine biofacies represented by the Rabbitkettle trilobites. Conodonts were examined to determine whether the sequences and composition of open shelf faunas from the Rabbitkettle have closer affinity to Miller's (1969, 1970, 1975, 1978) diverse carbonate platform conodont faunas or to Landing's (1978, 1979) coeval low diversity conodont faunas with restricted biostratigraphic utility from slope sequences.

This report contributes towards a biofacies evaluation of Cambrian-Ordovician boundary bed conodonts and illustrates the probable limitations on a highly resolved conodont-based correlation of this interval between strongly contrasting lithofacies.

Geologic Setting and Stratigraphy

Three formations of Late Cambrian and Early Ordovician age are exposed on the Mackenzie Platform, a stable tectonic element which received dominantly shallow-water sediments from the Helikian to the Late Devonian (Gabrielse, 1967): the Franklin Mountain Formation in the Mackenzie Valley (Norford and Macqueen, 1975), the Broken Skull Formation in the eastern and central Mackenzie Mountains (Gabrielse et al., 1973; Ludvigsen, 1975), and the Rabbitkettle Formation in the western Mackenzie Mountains and the Selwyn Mountains (Gabrielse et al., 1973).

These formations are poorly dated. Scattered fossil collections suggest that each spans the interval of, at least, Franconian to Canadian (Norford and Macqueen, 1975; Gabrielse et al., 1973; Ludvigsen, 1975; Tipnis et al., 1979).

The Rabbitkettle Formation comprises a thick sequence of grey weathering and banded silty limestones and calcareous siltstones near the border between the District of Mackenzie and Yukon Territory. Complete stratigraphic sections have not been located, but Gabrielse et al. (1973) suggested a minimum thickness of 1200 m for the Rabbitkettle in the Selwyn Mountains. Towards the east, the Rabbitkettle is replaced by silty and sandy, locally cross-bedded and pisolitic limestones and dolostones of the Broken Skull Formation which are, in turn, replaced by stromatolitic dolostones of the Franklin Mountain Formation further to the east.

Detailed biostratigraphic work on the upper Rabbitkettle Formation dates from 1972 when Ludvigsen measured a 750 m section of Upper Cambrian and Ordovician rocks near the headwaters of the Broken Skull River (Fig. 1). This section, designated Section K (Fig. 2), includes the upper Rabbitkettle Formation and the lower Road River Formation. A prominent black dolostone member overlying the Rabbitkettle was initially assigned to the lower Sunblood Formation and a significant hiatus was presumed to separate these units (Ludvigsen, 1975: fig. 7). However, Tipnis et al. (1979) demonstrated that Early Arenigian conodonts occur above the black dolostone member and that the hiatus, if indeed present, must be minor. This dolostone unit is herein considered to be a basal member of the Road River Formation.

3

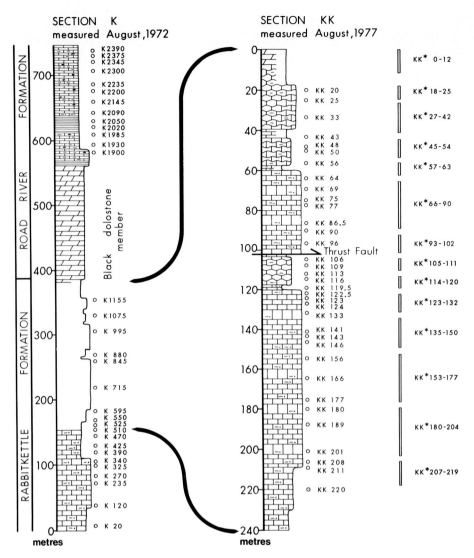

Fig. 2   Diagram of Section K showing the samples (K prefix) that yielded the conodonts discussed by Tipnis et al. (1979). When Section K was measured, it was considered to represent a continuous and structurally uncomplicated stratigraphic section. Detailed sampling of the upper 240 m of the Rabbitkettle Formation (Section KK) provided evidence of a thrust fault located 102 m below the top of the formation. Thus, the interval 44–102 m of the hanging wall corresponds to the interval 102–160 m of the foot wall. The position of samples dissolved in the search for conodonts is indicated (KK prefix). Also shown are the intervals represented by composite samples (KK* prefix).

The recovery of silicified trilobites at a number of levels below the black dolostone in Section K prompted a reinvestigation of this part of the section, and the upper 240 m of the Rabbitkettle was sampled in detail by Ludvigsen in 1977. This new section was designated Section KK (Fig. 2). Thirty-five bulk limestone samples, ranging in weight from 2 to more than 20 kg, were collected through the section. One and

4

Table 1 Conodont abundance in samples from the foot wall of Section KK (see Fig. 2)

	KK 211	KK 189	KK 180	KK 177	KK 166	KK 156	KK 146	KK 141	KK 133	KK 124	KK 123	KK 122.5	KK 119.5	KK 116	KK 113	KK 109	KK 106
Cordylodus oklahomensis																	
cordylodiform element										18					7		7
cytoniodiform element										10		1					2
Fryxellodontus? sp. nov.																	
serratus element							1										
"Proconodontus" carinatus																	
drepanodiform element				1		1		1					1				
scandodiform element				1		1											1
"Prooneotodus" tenuis																	
isolated element														1			
Phosphannulus universalis				1			1			1	1						1

5

Table 2 Conodont abundance in samples from the hanging wall of Section KK (see Fig. 2)

	KK 96	KK 90	KK 86.5	KK 78	KK 77	KK 75	KK 69	KK 64	KK 56	KK 53	KK 50	KK 48	KK 43	KK 33	KK 25	KK 20
Cordylodus intermedius s.f.														1		
Cordylodus oklahomensis cordylodiform element									1		3		7	59		
cyrtoniodiform element														12		
Furnishina asymmetrica s.f.														1		
Fryxellodontus inornatus symmetricus element													1			
"*Oneotodus*" *nakamurai*				1												
"*Proconodontus*" *carinatus* drepanodiform element	2		1	2					1				1	28		
scandodiform element			2										3	6		
Proconodontus serratus s.f.			2													
"*Prooneotodus*" *tenuis* isolated element			3		1				1							
three-element incomplete half-apparatus					1											
Phosphannulus universalis	1													4		

6

Table 3   Conodont abundance in productive composite samples from the foot and hanging walls of Section KK (see Fig. 2)

	KK* 135-150	KK* 45-54	KK* 27-42	KK* 0-12
Cordylodus oklahomensis				
cordylodiform element		1	2	
cyrtoniodiform element		1	3	
"Oneotodus" nakamurai	1			
"Proconodontus" carinatus				
drepanodiform element				
scandodiform element				1
Proconodontus serratus s.f.	1			
Protoconodont sp. indet. *s.f.*	2			
Phosphannulus universalis	1			

one-half to 2 kg of each sample were dissolved in acetic acid to recover conodonts; the remainder was dissolved in hydrochloric acid in the search for silicified trilobites. The samples are identified by a letter/number combination (e.g., KK 50) indicating the distance in metres below top of the Rabbitkettle Formation. In addition, a suite of hand samples, identified in the form of KK* 0–12 to indicate the stratigraphic interval represented by these composite samples, was processed to recover conodonts.

Examination of the sequence of silicified trilobites in Section KK led to the recognition that a 58 m interval in the upper Rabbitkettle Formation is repeated by a thrust fault which is located 102 m below the top of the formation (Fig. 2). The interval KK 44 to KK 102 of the hanging wall corresponds to the interval KK 102 to KK 160 of the foot wall of the thrust. The repeated interval includes the Cambrian-Ordovician boundary. The resulting composite Section KK (Fig. 3) shows the true stratigraphic thickness of the interval from KK 220 to the top of the Rabbitkettle to be about 160 m. In this paper, levels within the upper Rabbitkettle are cited as distances in metres below the top of the formation in the composite section.

Previous Investigations

Tipnis et al. (1979) outlined a conodont succession for Section K (Fig. 2). Biostratigraphically nondiagnostic Upper Cambrian conodonts were recovered from samples K 270 and K 390 (249 m and 213 m below the top of the Rabbitkettle Formation). *Proconodontus muelleri* Miller *s.f.* (= *sensu formo*) in K 525 (172 m below top of Rabbitkettle) represents some portion of Miller's (1975, 1977) *Proconodontus* Zone and suggests a possible early or middle Trempealeauan age. Similarly, their report of *"Oneotodus" nakamurai* Nogami, *"O.* cf. *O. datsonensis"* Druce and Jones and *"O. simplex"* (Furnish) (here regarded as *"O." nakamurai*), *Oistodus* cf. *cambricus*

7

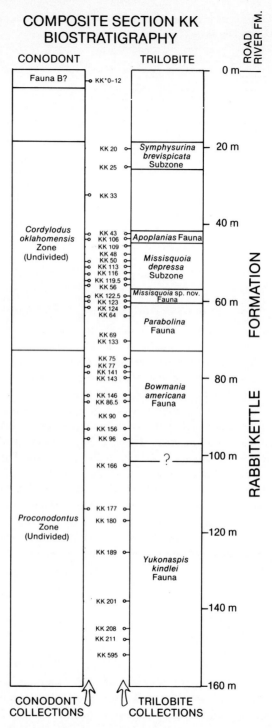

Fig. 3   Composite Section KK showing restored stratigraphic position of samples from the foot and hanging walls of the thrust fault. Productive conodont and trilobite samples are indicated, as are the stratal limits for the conodont and trilobite biostratigraphic units that are discussed in the text.

8

Miller *s.f.* and *Proconodontus* spp. *s.f.* in K 715 (112 m below top of Rabbitkettle) represents Miller's (1975, 1978) *Proconodontus notchpeakensis* or *Oistodus minutus* subzones of the *Proconodontus* Zone. This fauna indicates an equivalency with the upper *Saukiella junia* or *S. serotina* subzones of the *Saukia* Zone in Utah (Miller, 1978). *Cordylodus* spp. *s.f.* in association with *Missisquoia* Zone trilobites from K 880 (57 m below top of Rabbitkettle) represents the lowest Ordovician portion of Miller's (1975) *Cordylodus proavus* Zone.

An illustrated drepanodiform element, *Drepanodus* cf. *D. simplex* Furnish *s.f.*, with "*Oneotodus*" spp. from K 995 and unfigured platform elements from K 1150 (60 m and 25 m below top of Rabbitkettle) were respectively referred to Ethington and Clark's (1971) Fauna B (K 995) and the middle or upper Tremadocian (K 1150). The occurrence of North Atlantic lower Arenigian (K 1900), middle Arenigian (K 2020–K 2145), and upper Arenigian or Llanvirnian (K 2375) conodonts from the Road River Formation suggests that no significant unconformity is present above the Rabbitkettle Formation (Tipnis et al., 1979).

Trilobite Sequence

The lower 76 m of the composite section (KK 166 to KK 211 and K 510 to K 595 in the foot wall) is assigned to the *Yukonaspis kindlei* Fauna and is considered correlative to the *Saukiella junia* Subzone of Texas and Oklahoma. This correlation is based on the presence of *Euptychaspis typicalis* Ulrich, *Triarthropsis limbata* Rasetti, *Heterocaryon tuberculatum* Rasetti, *Rhaptagnostus clarki* (Kobayashi), and *Calvinella* cf. *prethoparia* Longacre as well as stratigraphic position below the superjacent biostratigraphic unit. This interval also includes species of *Richardsonella* (?), *Eurekia*, *Tatonaspis*, and a saukiid, as well as *Yukonaspis kindlei*.

The next 22 m in the composite section (KK 141 to KK 156 in the foot wall and KK 75 to KK 156 in the hanging wall) is assigned to the *Bowmania americana* Fauna. *Yukonaspis*, *Richardsonella* (?), *Idiomesus*, *Eurekia*, *Heterocaryon*, *Liostracinoides*, *Bowmania americana* (Walcott), and two new genera also occur in this fauna.

Overlying the *Bowmania americana* Fauna in the composite section is a 9 m interval assigned to the *Parabolina* Fauna (KK 124 to KK 133 in the foot wall and KK 64 in the hanging wall). This fauna includes *Parabolina* sp. nov., *Richardsonella* (?) cf. *quadrispinosa* Palmer, *Bienvillia* cf. *corax* (Billings), and "*Leiobienvillia*" *leonensis* Winston and Nicholls, in addition to species of *Yukonaspis*, *Geragnostus*, *Idiomesus*, *Eurekia*, and *Plethometopus*. A single specimen of *Missisquoia* occurs in KK 133. This fauna is correlated with the *Corbinia apopsis* Subzone of Texas and Oklahoma.

A narrow stratigraphic interval above the *Parabolina* Fauna in the foot wall (KK 122.5 and KK 123) contains a low diversity assemblage of *Missisquoia* sp. nov., *Parabolinella*, *Geragnostus*, and *Plethometopus*. This is named the *Missisquoia* sp. nov. Fauna. It is not certain whether this represents an older level than the base of the *Missisquoia* Zone in Oklahoma.

The next 12 m of the composite section (KK 109 to KK 119.5 in the foot wall and

9

KK 48 to KK 56 in the hanging wall) is confidently assigned to the *Missisquoia depressa* Subzone. This interval is very fossiliferous and contains *Parabolinella* sp. nov., *Parabolinella hecuba* (Walcott), *Missisquoia depressa* Stitt, *Ptychopleurites brevifrons* (Kobayashi), *Geragnostus, Levisaspis glabrus* (Shaw), and *Plethometopus*.

Overlying the *Missisquoia depressa* Subzone in the composite section is an interval (KK 106 in the foot wall and KK 43 in the hanging wall) dominated by *Parabolinella, Apoplanias,* and *Geragnostus*. This is named the *Apoplanias* Fauna and is tentatively correlated with the *Missisquoia typicalis* Subzone of Oklahoma.

The highest trilobite-bearing interval in the Rabbitkettle Formation is a narrow interval (KK 20 and KK 25 in the hanging wall) with *Apoplanias, Symphysurina* cf. *brevispicata* Hintze, and *Geragnostus*. These collections are correlated with the *S. brevispicata* Subzone of the *Symphysurina* Zone in Oklahoma.

Considerable problems are encountered in correlating the trilobite succession in the upper Rabbitkettle Formation at Section KK with coeval successions in central Texas (Winston and Nicholls, 1967; Longacre, 1970) and the Arbuckle and Wichita Mountains of Oklahoma (Stitt, 1971, 1977). Saukiid trilobites, the prime biostratigraphic indices of the Trempealeauan zonation established in Texas by Winston and Nicholls (1976) and Longacre (1970), are uncommon in the Rabbitkettle Formation. *Calvinella* is the only well-represented member of this family in Section KK and it only occurs in a single collection. Other important genera of the latest Cambrian zonation in Texas and Oklahoma, such as *Acheliops, Bayfieldia, Rasettia, Stenopilus, Theodenisia, Briscoia, Keithiella, Bynumina, Bynumiella,* and *Corbinia* have not been recovered from the Rabbitkettle Formation.

One of the few firm correlation tie-points between the Northwest Territories and Oklahoma (Fig. 4) is the 12 m thick *Missisquoia depressa* Subzone in the Rabbitkettle which undoubtedly is correlative with the 6 m thick *M. depressa* Subzone in the Signal Mountain Limestone in Oklahoma (Stitt, 1977). The substantial difference in generic composition within this subzone suggests the influence of environmental factors. The *M. depressa* Subzone in Oklahoma is strongly dominated by *Plethopeltis* (about 85% of 260 specimens). This genus does not occur in Section KK where the subzone is dominated by *Parabolinella* (about 65% of 760 specimens). *Geragnostus* is also much more abundant in the *M. depressa* Subzone in Section KK than in Oklahoma.

Each of the 14 trilobite collections from the base of the *Missisquoia* sp. nov. Fauna to the *Symphysurina* Zone at Section KK is dominated by olenid and agnostid trilobites. In addition, two olenids and one agnostid occur in the *Parabolina* Fauna. Thus, the upper part of Section KK is numerically dominated by trilobites characteristic of slope and outer shelf facies in the Lower Palaeozoic (Lochman-Balk and Wilson, 1958; Fortey, 1975; Taylor, 1977; Ludvigsen, 1979a). The evidence for the lower part of Section KK is less clear, but it is not inconsistent with a similar outer shelf position (Taylor, 1977:table 3). Section KK, therefore, records a sequence of trilobite faunas which, in comparison with coeval inner shelf sequences in Texas and Oklahoma, appears to represent an unrestricted open marine sequence deposited in an outer shelf setting.

10

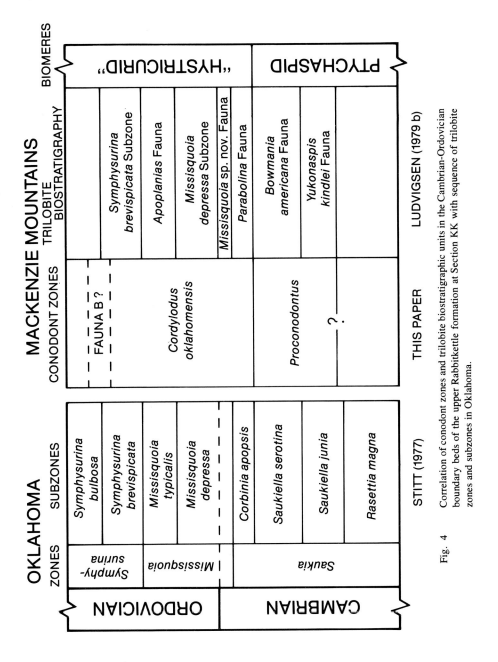

Fig. 4   Correlation of conodont zones and trilobite biostratigraphic units in the Cambrian-Ordovician boundary beds of the upper Rabbitkettle formation at Section KK with sequence of trilobite zones and subzones in Oklahoma.

11

Depositional Setting

Dark grey, thinly bedded, more-or-less silty lime mudstone and fossiliferous lime wackestone that regularly alternate with finely laminated, thinner calcareous siltstones dominate the section. Thin oolitic and granule intraclastic lime wackestones and packstones appear in the *Yukonaspis kindlei* Fauna and the *Bowmania americana* Fauna. Bedding surfaces are typically planar with sedimentary boundinage appearing with the *Parabolina* Fauna and through higher strata. Bioturbation and light grey lime wackestones and mudstones are present only in the *Bowmania americana* Fauna interval. Trilobite remains observed on bedding surfaces and in etched residues are typically disarticulated but are neither abraded nor severely broken.

The regular alternations of fine-grained silty, dark limestones and thinner calcareous siltstones with occasional well-sorted and winnowed allochem limestones suggest episodic deposition generally below effective wave base. The absence of features such as penecontemporaneously contorted and folded beds, slumps, mass movement deposits occupying channels, and carbonate flyschoid beds with erosional bases precludes deposition on or at the foot of a steep submarine slope. Such features appear in coeval fine-grained clastics of the Road River Formation in the Selwyn Basin to the northwest of Section K (Cecile, 1978).

Similarly, a restricted marine, very shallow or intertidal, inner shelf depositional environment is not indicated because of the absence of fenestral fabric, flat pebbles, channels and scour and fill structures, early dolomitized lime mudstone, prominent bioturbation, algalaminates and stromatolites, wave or tidally produced sedimentary structures, evaporites, and light coloration (Roehl, 1967; Shinn, 1968; Wilson, 1970, 1974; Cook, 1972).

The upper Rabbitkettle Formation of Section KK contains few lithologic features which can be assigned to a unique depositional environment. However, it is probable that these beds were deposited under low energy open shelf or very low angle muddy slope conditions. It is questionable whether Wilson's (1969) association of the type of sedimentary boudinage present within the Lower Ordovician of Section KK with shallow subtidal shelf deposition below effective wave base is appropriate. The presence of intercalated oolitic, intraclastic, and fossiliferous (trilobite and "pelmatozoan") grainstones and packstones low in the sequence suggests that lime mud and silt deposition was punctuated by the transport of allochthonous carbonate debris by nonturbid bottom traction currents or nonturbid sand sheet flows. The source of this debris quite likely lay to the east in the area of platform deposition of the Broken Skull Formation.

A two-fold division is apparent in the rocks of Section KK: 1) a lower sequence of planar bedded, medium to light grey and silty lime mudstones, wackestones, and grainstones, which locally are bioturbed, and 2) an upper sequence of wavy bedded, dark grey and silty lime mudstones which lack bioturbation. This lithologic division also coincides with a pronounced fanual division. The lower sequence (*Yukonaspis kindlei* Fauna and *Bowmania americana* Fauna) contains typical *Saukia* Zone trilobites and the upper sequence (*Parabolina* Fauna to *Symphysurina brevispicata* Subzone) is dominated by olenids, agnostids, and trilobites of probable extra-North American origin. The base of the *Parabolina* Fauna thus coincides with a significant environmental change and this level was interpreted by Ludvigsen (1979b) as a biomere boundary.

Conodont Sequence

General

Ten multi-element and form species are represented among the 202 specimens recovered from 23 of 45 samples. Conodont elements have a thermal colour alteration index of 4.5 to 5 (Epstein et al., 1977) and slightly corroded surfaces. The sparse, low diversity conodont faunas from Section KK can be compared with Miller's (1975, 1977, 1978) conodont zonation of the western USA.

Proconodontus Zone

Conodonts from the upper *Yukonaspis kindlei* Fauna and *Bowmania americana* Fauna intervals of Section KK include multi-element *"Proconodontus" carinatus* Miller (= *Proconodontus carinatus s.f.* and *P. notchpeakensis* Miller *s.f.*), *P. serratus* Miller *s.f.*, *"Oneotodus" nakamurai* Nogami, *"Prooneotodus" tenuis* (Müller), and *Furnishina asymmetrica* Müller.

Miller (1978) has equated the upper *Saukiella junia* Subzone and lowest *S. serotina* Subzone with the *Proconodontus notchpeakensis* Subzone of the *Proconodontus* Zone. The first appearance of *Oistodus minutus* Miller *s.f.* in the lower *S. serotina* Subzone and its persistence to the top of that trilobite subzone defines the *Oistodus minutus* Subzone of the upper *Proconodontus* Zone.

Oistodus minutus s.f. was not recovered in this study. Consequently, the faunally similar *Proconodontus notchpeakensis* and *O. minutus* subzones cannot be differentiated in Section KK.

"Oneotodus" nakamurai appears in the *Bowmania americana* Fauna in Section KK. The species has its lowest occurrence in the *Corbinia apopsis* Subzone in the western United States where it regularly appears along with the first *Cordylodus* form species (Miller, 1975, 1977, 1978; Kurtz, 1976). However, *"O." nakamurai* occurs in rocks older than those bearing *Cordylodus* in the People's Republic of China (Nogami, 1967), Alberta (Derby et al., 1972), Appalachian North America (Landing, 1977, 1979), Korea (Lee, 1975), and Australia (Druce and Jones, 1971).

A single element representing *Fryxellodontus*? sp. nov. from the *Bowmania americana* Fauna is a possible Upper Cambrian representative of the genus. *Fryxellodontus lineatus* Miller and *F. inornatus* Miller first appear at the base of the Lower Ordovician *Missisquoia typicalis* Subzone in the western United States (Miller, 1977, 1978).

Tipnis et al. (1979) report an anomalous occurrence of *Clavohamulus* cf. *C. bulbousus* (Miller) from K 390 (213 m below the top of the Rabbitkettle). The species is known from the upper *Missisquoia typicalis* Subzone and lower *Symphysurina* Zone in the western USA (Miller, 1978). The occurrence of the species below the lowest studied trilobites in Section KK (*Yukonaspis kindlei* Fauna) suggests that the *Clavohamulus* lineage originated considerably before the Lower Ordovician.

13

Cordylodus oklahomensis Zone

The disappearance of several conodont species and the appearance of *Cordylodus proavus* Müller *s.f.*, *C. oklahomensis* Müller *s.f.*, *"Oneotodus" nakamurai*, and *Hirsutodontus* at the base of the *Corbinia apopsis* Subzone define the base of Miller's (1975, 1977, 1978) *Cordylodus proavus* Zone. Miller (1975, 1977, 1978) has divided the latest Cambrian through lowest Ordovician *Cordylodus proavus* Zone (= *Corbinia apopsis* Subzone– lower *Symphysurina* Zone) into five subzones.

Cordylodus proavus s.f. is part of multi-element *C. oklahomensis* (see Systematic Palaeontology) and the designation *"Cordylodus oklahomensis* Zone" is here substituted for *"C. proavus* Zone".

Cordylodus oklahomensis Zone faunas from Section KK are sparse and of low diversity. The eponymous species first appears in uppermost Cambrian strata equivalent to the *Corbinia apopsis* Subzone although the species was not recovered in this study from the base of the *Parabolina* Fauna. However, the *Proconodontus* and *C. oklahomensis* Zone faunas are not as strongly differentiated as they are in Texas, Utah, and Wyoming (Miller, 1975, 1977, 1978; Kurtz, 1976). As noted above, *"Oneotodus" nakamurai* first appears in the *Proconodontus* Zone in the Rabbitkettle. In addition, Tipnis et al. (1979) note the co-occurrence of *Proconodontus muelleri* Miller *s.f.* with *Cordylodus proavus s.f.* and *Missisquoia* in K 880 (57 m below top of Rabbitkettle Formation). The persistence of *P. muelleri* into the Lower Ordovician contrasts with the species' disappearance just below the *Corbinia apopsis* Subzone in the western USA (Miller, 1975, 1977, 1978; Kurtz, 1976). *Proconodontus* Zone species also persist into the local range zone of *Cordylodus oklahomensis* in Vermont (Landing, 1979).

Miller's subzonal sequence of the *Cordylodus oklahomensis* Zone is based on the range zones of species of *Hirsutodontus, Clavohamulus,* and *Fryxellodontus.* The absence of these forms precludes division of the zone in Section KK. A single element of *Fryxellodontus inornatus* from KK 43 supports the tentative correlation of the *Apoplanias* Fauna with the *Missisquoia typicalis* Subzone. Miller (1978) documents the occurrence of *F. inornatus* through the *Fryxellodontus inornatus* and lower *Clavohamulus* subzones (middle *Cordylodus oklahomensis* Zone) and equates these with the *Missisquoia typicalis* Subzone.

The youngest conodont collection (KK* 0–12) consists of one element of *"Proconodontus" carinatus.* This composite sample was collected above the highest trilobite collection (KK 20) and could represent either the upper *Cordylodus oklahomensis* Zone or Ethington and Clark's (1971) Fauna B. This uncertain correlation is due to the absence of associated *Cordylodus* form species. Fauna B is recognized by the appearance of advanced form species of *Cordylodus,* including *Cordylodus lindstromi* Druce and Jones, 1971, and *C. intermedius* Furnish, 1938 (Miller, 1975). However, 1) the recovery of *C. intermedius* from the *Cordylodus oklahomensis* Zone (Miller, 1978; Landing, 1979; this report), 2) the probability that *"C. lindstromi"* is an ontogenetic variant with supernumerary basal tips that appears in all *Cordylodus* elements (Landing, 1979), and 3) the persistence of upper *Cordylodus oklahomensis* Zone species into Fauna B (Miller, 1970; Landing, 1979) make the differentiation of Fauna B unclear at present.

14

Conodont Biofacies

Although conodonts are sparsely represented in samples from Section KK, the faunal sequence has closer similarities with continental slope sequences from the Appalachians (Landing, 1979) than with inner carbonate platform successions in the western USA (Miller, 1969, 1970, 1975, 1977, 1978; Kurtz, 1976). These differences are most obvious in the generic composition of the euconodont components (Bengtson, 1976) of *Cordylodus oklahomensis* Zone faunas.

Multi-element *"Proconodontus" carinatus* and *Cordylodus oklahomensis* and mono-elemental *"Oneotodus" nakamurai* are dominant species both in continental slope and inner carbonate platform sequences. These three species are represented by 83 per cent of the elements from Miller's (1978) Lava Dam Five section in the upper Notch Peak Limestone and lower House Limestone, western Utah. Species of *Clavohamulus, Fryxellodontus,* and *Hirsutodontus*, which are used for the subzonation of the *Cordylodus oklahomensis* Zone (Miller, 1975), are represented by 7 per cent of the elements at the Lava Dam Five section. Although elements of *Clavohamulus, Fryxellodontus*, and *Hirsutodontus* are relatively minor components of *Cordylodus oklahomensis* Zone faunas in shallow-water sequences, these components are absent or very sparingly represented in continental slope deposits in the Appalachians. Landing (1979) recovered only one element of *Fryxellodontus lineatus* from the Highgate and Gorge formations, northwestern Vermont. Similarly, representatives of the three genera have not been encountered in *Cordylodus oklahomensis* Zone faunas from the Green Point Group, western Newfoundland (E. Landing, unpublished data). Similar *Cordylodus oklahomensis* Zone faunas are present in the lower Grove Formation, at Lime Kiln, central Maryland (E. Landing, unpublished data) where the transition from the upper Frederick Limestone to the lower Grove Formation represents a progradation of shallow shelf carbonates over fine-grained carbonates (Reinhardt, 1974). The lower Grove Formation at Lime Kiln consists of festoon bedded, oolite bar deposits. This shelf margin sequence has yielded low diversity conodont faunas comprised of *Cordylodus, "Proconodontus"*, and *"Oneotodus"*.

The reasons for the absence or near absence of *Clavohamulus, Fryxellodontus*, and *Hirsutodontus* from the outermost shelf or slope environments listed above and from the Rabbitkettle Formation are unknown. Water depth and energy of the environment do not seem to be common factors which would limit their distribution. It is possible that representatives of the three genera were adapted to variable and/or elevated salinities and temperatures of the restricted marine conditions of the inner shelf and were environmentally stenotopic. *Cordylodus* species and the ancestral *"Proconodontus" carinatus* and *"Oneotodus" nakamurai* are geographically widespread in terms of lithofacies associations and were presumably eurytopic.

Biofacies developments in euconodont distributions in *Proconodontus* Zone faunas are obscure at present. Landing (1979) did not encounter *Oistodus minutus* Miller *s.f.* in upper *Proconodontus* Zone faunas in slope deposits in northwestern Vermont. The form was recovered in turbiditic limestones in the Taconic allochthon (Landing, 1977, 1979) although it is absent in the uppermost Cambrian in the Green Point Group, western Newfoundland (E. Landing, unpublished data). Similarly, deep shelf lithotopes of the uppermost Frederick Limestone, central Maryland, have not yielded the species. It is possible that *O. minutus* may be found to be more regularly associated with restricted, marine inner shelf deposits.

15

Discussion

Reinvestigation of the lithologic and faunal sequences of Section KK demonstrates the stratigraphic repetition of the section by a thrust fault located 102 m below the top of the Rabbitkettle Formation. Tipnis et al. (1979) recovered lowest Ordovician conodonts and trilobites at K 880 (Fig. 2). Conodonts from their sample K 995 higher in the section do not represent Ethington and Clark's (1971) Fauna B and are referable to the preuppermost Cambrian *Proconodontus* Zone (*Saukiella serotina* Subzone equivalent). Similarly, the report of middle or upper Tremadocian "platform elements" from K 1150 (30.4 m below top of Rabbitkettle) (Tipnis et al. 1979) cannot be evaluated because the specimens were not illustrated. However, conodonts recovered in this study from KK 33 and KK* 0–12 seem to represent the upper *Cordylodus oklahomensis* Zone or, possibly, Fauna B, and are of Lower Tremadocian aspect.

As discussed above, the Rabbitkettle Formation at Section KK has no lithologic features indicating shallow, inner carbonate platform deposition. The deep, outer shelf or low angle slope depositional environment suggested above is supported by the composition of uppermost Cambrian and lowest Ordovician trilobite faunas.

The absence of *Clavohamulus* and *Hirsutodontus* and poor representation of *Fryxellodontus* in *Cordylodus oklahomensis* Zone faunas from the Rabbitkettle Formation at Section KK are considered to be related to unrestricted marine conditions of deposition and have parallels in Appalachian outermost shelf and continental slope faunas. Although it is less clear, the absence of *Oistodus minutus s.f.* in the upper *Proconodontus* Zone may also be related to the palaeogeographic setting of Section KK.

Miller's (1975, 1977, 1978) conodont-based subzonation of the uppermost Cambrian through lowest Ordovician (*Saukiella junia* Subzone through lower *Symphysurina* Zone) provides a biostratigraphic resolution comparable to that provided by trilobite faunas. However, the absence of key conodont species in Cambrian-Ordovician boundary beds in outer shelf and slope deposits results in recognition only of the *Proconodontus* and *Cordylodus oklahomensis* zones and not faunas referable to conodont subzones. This biofacies control of conodonts has probable implications for conodont-based correlations of Cambrian-Ordovician (Olenidian-Tremadocian series) boundary beds of the classic Acado-Baltic biofacies of the Cambrian and Ordovician systems. The deposition of the carbonate-poor Acado-Baltic sequences of this age in palaeogeographic settings that had unrestricted access to the open ocean (Ross, 1975) suggests that conodont species required for subzonation of the *Proconodontus* and *Cordylodus oklahomensis* zones may not be encountered here with enough regularity for precise correlations. Landing et al. (1978) recovered only *Proconodontus carinatus s.f.* and *Cordylodus proavus s.f.* in the uppermost Cambrian in the Acado-Baltic sequence on Navy Island, New Brunswick, and did not encounter the *Hirsutodontus* species which appear in the lowest *Cordylodus oklahomensis* Zone in the western USA (see also Miller, 1977, 1978).

16

Systematic Palaeontology

Remarks

Conodont taxa are listed alphabetically. A suprageneric classification is not applied although the informal designations "protoconodont", "paraconodont", and "euconodont" (Bengtson, 1976) are used to summarize the growth modes of conodont elements. Conodont form species are designated in *sensu formo (s.f.)* when the composition of the apparatus is unknown. The presumed hyolithelminthoid *Phosphannulus* is listed at the end of the section.

Repository

Royal Ontario Museum, Toronto (ROM). Figured specimens are stored under ROM numbers 38361 to 38375. Topotype collections from the upper Rabbitkettle Formation are reposited under ROM numbers 38401 to 38444.

Phylum uncertain
Class uncertain
Order Conodontophorida Eichenberg, 1930

Genus *Cordylodus* Pander, 1856

Type Species

Cordylodus angulatus Pander, 1856, *s.f.* from the Early Ordovician glauconitic sandstones of Estonia.

Emended Diagnosis

Euconodonts represented by a bi-elemental apparatus consisting of a numerically predominant cordylodiform element and a subordinate cyrtoniodiform element. Cusp and denticles are albid and the elements lack any surface microsculpture.

Discussion

Previous reconstructions of the *Cordylodus* apparatus (Bergström and Sweet, 1966; Sweet and Bergström, 1972; Barnes and Poplawski, 1973; Nowlan, 1976) are not followed in this report and J. F. Miller's (pers. comm. to E. L., 1977) reconstruction is followed. The *Cordylodus* apparatus is bi-elemental and consists of an element with rounded denticles and cusp and a second element with laterally flattened, basally confluent denticles and cusp. The former, termed the "rounded element" by Miller, is here designated the "cordylodiform element" because this plan is shown by the type form species. The second element, Miller's "flattened element", is termed the "cyrtoniodiform element" because its plan is similar enough to *Cyrtoniodus* Stauffer *s.f.* that some authors (Miller, 1970; Ethington and Clark, 1971) have referred "flattened elements" to that form genus.

Cordylodiform elements are generally more abundant in collections than cyrtonio-diform elements. The former are more variable in a large collection than associated cyrtoniodiform elements and show a more-or-less distinctive symmetry transition series (see also Ethington and Clark, 1971 : 68, pl. 1, figs. 15, 16, 20). Cordylodiform elements designated in the literature as 1) *Cordylodus proavus* Müller *s.f.*, 2) *C. intermedius* Furnish *s.f.*, and 3) *"C. lindstromi"* Druce and Jones *s.f.* are externally identical. They are separable, respectively, by 1) a convex anterior margin of the basal cavity, 2) a straight to concave anterior margin of the basal cavity, and 3) convex to concave anterior profile of the basal cavity and presence of secondary basal tips. The associated cyrtoniodiform elements are 1) *C. oklahomensis* Müller, *s.f.*, 2) an unnamed element often misidentified as *C. oklahomensis* or *C. prion* Lindström *s.f.* and 3) an element included by Druce and Jones (1971) in the definition of *"C. lindstromi"* *s.f.* These cyrtoniodiform elements are distinguished by developments in the anterior profile of the basal cavity which parallel those in the cordylodiform element.

"Cordylodus lindstromi" elements are not considered to represent a biologic species. Druce and Jones (1971) illustrated a cyrtoniodiform holotype (pl. 1, figs. 9a, b, text-fig. 23h) and paratype cordylodiform (pl. 1, figs. 7a–8b, pl. 2, figs. 8a–c) elements with secondary basal tips. One paratype (pl. 2, figs. 8a–c) has a convex anterior margin of the basal cavity and is comparable to *C. proavus s.f.* with exception of a second basal tip. A second paratype (pl. 1, figs. 7a, b) has the straight anterior margin of the basal cavity which is present in early elements of *C. intermedius.* Druce and Jones's (1971) holotype of *"C. lindstromi"* is otherwise comparable to the cyrtoniodiform element of *Cordylodus intermedius.* Miller (1970) illustrated in *nomen nudum* forms designated *Cordylodus insertus* sp. nov. *s.f.* and *C.* sp. aff. *insertus* sp. nov. *s.f.* These elements are closely similar to *C. proavus s.f.* and *C. oklahomensis s.f.*, respectively, but have an additional basal tip.

Accessory apices of the basal cavity are regarded in this report as not of significance in the classification of *Cordylodus* and are developmental variants. The anterior profile of the basal cavity is considered to have primary significance in the classification of *Cordylodus* elements. Although Miller (1975, 1977) has used the first appearance of *"Cordylodus lindstromi"* in defining Ethington and Clark's Fauna B, he has illustrated a *C. oklahomensis s.f.* element from the underlying *Cordylodus oklahomensis* Zone with secondary apices of the basal cavity (Miller, 1969: pl. 65, fig. 53). Nowlan (1976) recovered *"C. lindstromi"* from sequences older than Fauna B.

Advanced *Cordylodus intermedius* gave rise to multi-element *C. angulatus* Pander and *C. rotundatus* Pander of Fauna C. The latter apparatuses have apparently indistinguishable cyrtoniodiform elements referable to *C. prion* Lindström *s.f.* (J. F. Miller, pers. comm. to E. L., 1977). The "phrygian cap" anterior profile of the basal cavity of *C. angulatus s.f.* and *C. rotundatus s.f.* is a more exaggerated condition than that seen in the concave profile of *C. intermedius s.f.*

Cordylodus is a characteristic latest Cambrian and Tremadocian genus in the North American, Australasian, Siberian, and Acado-Baltic faunal provinces (Müller, 1959, 1973; Miller, 1969; Druce and Jones, 1971; Abaimova and Markov, 1977; Landing, et al., 1978). Van Wamel (1974) reported the genus in the lower Arenigian of Sweden. Dzik (1976) renamed a Llanvirnian and Llandeilian apparatus containing cordylodiform and ramiform elements *Spinodus spinatus* (Hadding). *Cordylodus horridus*

18

s.f. of Barnes and Poplawski (1973) from the uppermost Arenigian (Landing, 1976) seems to be part of an undescribed apparatus (R. L. Ethington, pers. comm. to E. L. 1978).

The ancestor of the earliest appearing *Cordylodus* species, *Cordylodus oklahomensis,* appears to have been a middle Trempealeauan species consisting of *Proconodontus carinatus* Miller *s.f.* and *P. notchpeakensis* Miller *s.f.*

Cordylodus intermedius **Furnish, 1938,** *s.f.*
Figs. 5E, 6A, B

Cordylodus intermedius Furnish, 1938:338, pl. 42, fig. 31, text-fig. 2C.
Cordylodus insertus Miller, 1970:88, 89 *(nomen nudum) (pars,* pl. 1, figs. 37, 38).
Cordylodus cf. *C. angulatus*—Druce and Jones, 1971:67, text-fig. 23c.
Cordylodus caseyi Druce and Jones, 1971:67, 68, pl. 2, figs. 9a–12c, text-figs. 23d, e.
Cordylodus intermedius—Druce and Jones, 1971:68, pl. 3, figs. 1a–3b, text-figs. 23f, g.
Cordylodus proavus—Druce and Jones, 1971:70, 71, *(pars,* pl. 1, figs. 1a, b, 3, 5a-6, text-figs. 23p, q, *(non C. proavus* Müller, 1959, *s.f.*).
Cordylodus cf. *C. proavus*—Druce and Jones, 1971:71, *(pars,* pl. 1, figs. 10a–11b, *non C. proavus* Müller, 1959, *s.f.*).
Cordylodus caseyi—Jones, 1971:46, pl. 2, figs. 1a–c.
Cordylodus intermedius—Jones, 1971:46, pl. 2, figs. 2a–3c.
Cordylodus lindstromi—Jones, 1971:47, pl. 2, figs. 4a–c.
Cordylodus intermedius—Müller, 1973:30, pl. 10, figs. 1a–3, text-figs. 2c, 4a, b.
Cordylodus lenzi Müller, 1973:31, pl. 10, figs. 5–9, text-figs. 2f, 5a, b.
Cordylodus angulatus—Viira, 1974:63, *(pars,* pl. 1, fig. 8, text-figs. 4a, b, *non C. angulatus Pander,* 1856, *s.f.*).
Cordylodus angulatus—van Wamel, 1974:58, 59, *(pars,* pl. 1, figs. 6, 7, *non C. angulatus* Pander, 1856, *s.f.*).
Cordylodus intermedius—Repetski, 1975:44, 45, pl. 1, figs. 11, 12.
Cordylodus intermedius—Nowlan, 1976:149, 150, pl. 2, figs. 1, 2.
?Cordylodus cf. *C. intermedius*—Tipnis et al., 1979:31, pl. 1, fig. 7.
Cordylodus intermedius—Landing, 1979:62–64, 133–135, 200–201, pl. II–3, fig. 3, pl. III–1, fig. 8, pl. IV–2, fig. 6 *(pars,* citations listed are only those of *C. intermedius s.f.*).

Occurrence and Hypotype

One element (ROM 38373) from KK 33. The associated conodont fauna represents the upper *Cordylodus oklahomensis* Zone.

Remarks

The shape of the basal cavity of *Cordylodus intermedius s.f.* is intermediate between those of *C. proavus s.f.* and *C. angulatus s.f.* as noted by Druce and Jones (1971) and

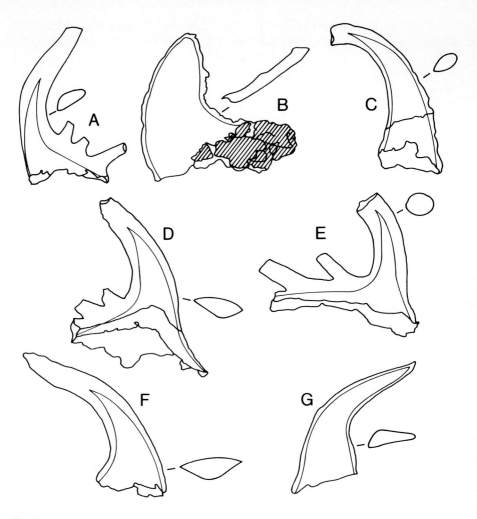

Fig. 5A, D   *Cordylodus oklahomensis* Müller, cordylodiform, ROM 38372, ×70, and cyrtoniodiform, ROM 38367, ×75, elements, respectively.

     B   *Fryxellodontus?* sp. nov. Lateral view of serrrated elements with attached pyrite crystals (diagonal ruling), ROM 38366, ×60.

     C, F   *"Proconodontus" carinatus* Miller, drepanodiform, ROM 38365, ×60, and scandodiform, ROM 38362, ×150, element, respectively.

     E   *Cordylodus intermedius* Furnish *s.f.*, ROM 38373, ×140.

     G   Protoconodont sp. indet. *s.f.*, ROM 38375, ×55.

Müller (1973). The element (Fig. 6A) has rounded denticles and cusp and has a straight anterior profile of the basal cavity which differs from the convex profile present in cordylodiform elements of *C. oklahomensis*. The surface of the element has undergone slight dissolution and blocky crystallites are exposed on the surface (Fig. 6B).

Cordylodus oklahomensis Müller, 1959
Figs. 5A, D, 6C–E

Cordylodiform Element

Cordylodus proavus Müller, 1959:448, 449, pl. 15, figs. 11, 12, 18, text-fig. 3B.
Cordylodus proavus—Miller, 1969:424–426, pl. 65, figs. 37–45, text-fig. 3D.
Cordylodus insertus Miller, 1970:88, 89 *(nomen nudum)*, *(pars,* pl. 1, fig. 37, text-fig. 11B).
Cordylodus proavus—Miller, 1970:89, text-fig. 11D.
Cordylodus lindstromi Druce and Jones, 1971:68, 69, pl. 2, figs. 8a–c *(pars)*.
Cordylodus proavus—Druce and Jones, 1971:70, 71 *(pars,* pl. 1, figs. 2a, b, 4a, b, text-fig. 23r).
Cordylodus cf. *C. proavus*—Druce and Jones, 1971:71, *(pars,* pl. 1, figs. 12a, b, text-fig. 23s).
Cordylodus proavus—Ethington and Clark, 1971:71, pl. 1, fig. 19.
Cordylodus proavus—Jones, 1971:48, pl. 2, figs. 9a–c.
Cordylodus proavus—Miller and Melby, 1971:120, pl. 1, figs. 18, 19.
Cordylodus proavus—Müller, 1973:35, pl. 9, figs. 1–4, 9, text-figs. 2a, 9a, b.
Cordylodus angulatus—van Wamel, 1974:58, 59 *(pars,* pl. 1, fig. 5, *non C. angulatus* Pander, 1856, *s.f.*).
Cordylodus proavus—Abaimova, 1975:109, 110, pl. 10, fig. 16, text-fig. 8 (27, 28).
Cordylodus proavus—Nowlan, 1974:15, pl. 1, figs. 9, 10, 14–16.
Cordylodus proavus—Abaimova and Markov, 1977:91, pl. 14, fig. 1.
Cordylodus proavus—Landing et al., 1978:76, text-fig. 2F.
Cordylodus proavus—Fåhraeus and Nowlan, 1978:453, pl. 1, figs. 8, 9.
Cordylodus proavus—Tipnis et al., 1979:31, pl. 1, figs. 8, 9.
?Cordylodus cf. *C. proavus*—Tipnis et al., 1979:31, pl. 1, fig. 10.
Cordylodus proavus—Landing, 1979:21, 22, pl. I-1, figs. 10, 13.
Cordylodus oklahomensis—Landing, 1979:64, 65, 135, 136, 202, 203, pl. II–3, fig. 1, pl. III–1, fig. 11, pl. IV–2, fig. 8 *(pars,* cited figures only of *C. proavus s.f.*).

Cyrtoniodiform Element

Cordylodus oklahomensis Müller, 1959:447, 448, pl. 15, figs. 15a–16.
Cordylodus oklahomensis—Miller, 1969:423, 424, pl. 65, figs. 46–53.
Cordylodus sp. aff. *C. insertus* Miller, 1970:89, pl. 1, fig. 40, text-fig. 11C.
Cyrtoniodus oklahomensis—Miller, 1970:90, 91, pl. 1, figs. 35, 36, text-fig. 11F.
non Cordylodus oklahomensis—Druce and Jones, 1971:69, pl. 5, figs. 6a–7c, text-fig. 23 (⁻ cyrtoniodiform element of *Cordylodus intermedius* Furnish apparatus).
Cordylodus oklahomensis—Ethington and Clark, 1971:71, pl. 1, fig. 24.
Cyrtoniodus prion—Miller and Melby, 1971:120 *(pars,* pl. 2, fig. 17, *non C. prion* Lindström, 1955, s.f.).
?Cordylodus oklahomensis—Jones, 1971:47, 48, pl. 2, figs. 5a–8b.
Cordylodus oklahomensis—Müller, 1973:33, pl. 9, figs. 12–13b, text-figs. 2B, 7a, b.

21

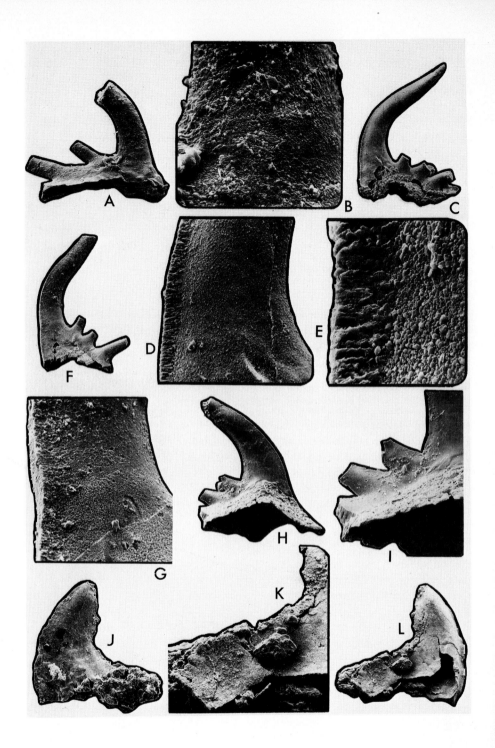

Cordylodus prion prion Nowlan, 1976:154–156, pl. 2, figs. 23–31.
Cordylodus oklahomensis—Landing, 1979:64, 65, 135, 136, pl. II–3, fig. 5, pl. III–1, fig. 10.

Occurrence

A total of 105 cordylodiform and 29 cyrtoniodiform elements from the uppermost Cambrian and lowest Ordovician of Section KK (*Parabolina* Fauna through *Apoplanias* Fauna).

Hypotypes

Cordylodiform elements ROM 38371 and ROM 38372 from KK 124 and cyrtoniodiform element ROM 38367 from KK 122.5.

Description

The component form species *Cordylodus proavus* and *C. oklahomensis* have been adequately redescribed by Miller (1969) and only remarks are presented here. Cordylodiform elements have discrete denticles and cusp which have well rounded to laterally flattened cross sections. A rounded carina may be present on the anterior and posterior edges of the cusp (Figs. 6C–G), and the anterior margin may be laterally deflected (Figs. 6F, G). Cyrtoniodiform elements have basally confluent denticles and, generally, a lateral flaring of the base under the cusp (Figs. 6H, I).

Crystallites present in *Cordylodus* elements apparently are oriented radially to the surface of the element. Edges or keels are formed by the elongation of these crystallites along the anterior margin of the cusp (Figs. 6C–G).

Fig. 6A, B   *Cordylodus intermedius* Furnish *s.f.*, ROM 38373, sample KK 33.
      A   Lateral view, ×120.
      B   Detail of slightly etched surface, ×602.
   C-E   *Cordylodus oklahomensis* Müller, cordylodiform element, ROM 38371, sample KK 124.
      C   Lateral view, ×60.
      D, E Detail of anterior carina showing orientation of crystallites, ×301 and ×1204, respectively.
   F, G   *Cordylodus oklahomensis* Müller, cordylodiform element, ROM 38372, sample KK 124.
      F   Lateral view of asymmetrical element, ×60.
      G   Detail of slightly etched surface and anterior carina, ×301.
   H, I   *Cordylodus oklahomensis* Müller, cyrtoniodiform element, ROM 38367, sample KK 122.5.
      H   Inner lateral view of element with attached basal plate, ×65.
      I   Detail showing contrasting surface texture of smooth conodont element and porous basal plate, ×129.
   J-L   *Fryxellodontus?* sp. nov., serrated element, ROM 38366, sample KK 146.
      J, L Lateral views, ×52.
      K   Right-lateral view showing denticulated oral edge of broken distal end of posterior process, ×103.

Remarks

Cordylodus proavus s.f. and *C. oklahomensis s.f.* are considered to be the component form species of multi-element *C. oklahomensis*. The two form species have a comparable stratigraphic range (Miller, 1969:426). Both elements appear at the same stratigraphic level in Utah (Miller, 1978) and Vermont (Landing, 1979), and co-occur in the same samples in Iran (Müller, 1973). The two form species also have nearly coincident ranges in Alberta (Derby et al., 1972) with *C. oklahomensis s.f.* first recovered less than a metre above the lowest occurrence of *C. proavus s.f.* Similarly, *C. proavus s.f.* and *"C. prion prion"* (= *C. oklahomensis s.f.*) of Nowlan (1976) first appear at the same level in the Copes Bay Formation in the Canadian Arctic and have similar stratigraphic ranges.

Druce and Jones (1971, see also Druce, 1978) described a stratigraphic overlap of *Cordylodus oklahomensis s.f.* only in the upper portion of the local range zone of *C. proavus s.f.* However, this stratigraphic non-concordance is probably related to the small number of specimens recovered. The illustrated specimens of *C. oklahomensis s.f.* from Australia (Druce and Jones, 1971) are apparently the cyrtoniodiform elements of multi-element *C. intermedius*.

Proconodontus notchpeakensis s.f. and *P. carinatus s.f.* are the apparent "ancestors", respectively, of *Cordylodus proavus s.f.* and *C. oklahomensis s.f.* (Miller, 1969, 1970). The similarity of the elements in bi-element *"Proconodontus" carinatus* (discussed below) to those of multi-element *C. oklahomensis* also suggests a comparable apparatus construction in the two species.

Cordylodus proavus s.f. appears to have been numerically dominant over *C. oklahomensis s.f.* in the *C. oklahomensis* apparatus. Miller (1978) recovered the elements in the ratio 3287:781 at the Lava Dam North section in Utah. A closely similar ratio 105:29 occurs in the Rabbitkettle collection. These data suggest that the elements occurred in the ratio 4:1 in a *C. oklahomensis* apparatus and that a minimum number of 10 elements was present in a bilaterally symmetrical *C. oklahomensis* animal.

Genus *Fryxellodontus* Miller, 1969

Type Species

Fryxellodontus inornatus Miller, 1969, from the Notch Peak Limestone, House Range, west-central Utah.

Fryxellodontus inornatus Miller, 1969
Figs. 7C–G

Fryxellodontus inornatus Miller, 1969:426, 428, 429, pl. 65, figs. 1–10, 12–16, 23–25, text-figs. 4A, C, D, E *(pars)*.
Fryxellodontus inornatus—Miller, 1970:97, text-figs. 10Q–T.
Gen. et sp. indet. B Druce and Jones, 1971:102, pl. 12, figs. 9a, b, text-fig. 33.
Fryxellodontus inornatus—Nowlan, 1976:237, pl. 1, figs. 17–19.

Occurrence and Hypotype

One *symmetricus* element (ROM 38368) from the *Apoplanias* Fauna, sample KK 43.

Remarks

Miller (1969) has provided a thorough description of the elements of the *Fryxellodontus inornatus* apparatus. An additional observation is that the elements lack surficial microsculpture when examined with the scanning electron microscope (Fig. 7C, D, G).

The element recovered from Section KK is composed of acicular crystallites oriented perpendicular to the surface of the specimen (Fig. 7E, F).

Fryxellodontus? sp. nov.
Fig. 5B, 6J–L, 7A, B

Occurrence and Hypotype

One element (ROM 38366) from the *Bowmania americana* Fauna (KK 146).

Description

A strongly laterally flattened, completely hollow, sheathlike element with a denticulated posterior process which is much longer than the blunt cusp. A smooth, open arc is formed by the posterior edge of the cusp and the oral edge. Lateral displacement of the anterior keel and slight concavity of the right-lateral surface produce asymmetry in the element.

Remarks

The element is completely hollow and lacks any surface microsculpture. It has some similarity to the *planus* and *serratus* elements of *Fryxellodontus inornatus* (Miller, 1969) although a long posterior process is present. This posterior process, which was broken in preparation, is distally denticulated (Fig. 6K, L).

It is uncertain whether the element actually represents a species of *Fryxellodontus* because associated elements of the apparatus were not recovered. However, if the element does belong to the genus, it is the only known Upper Cambrian representative of the genus.

Genus *Furnishina* Müller, 1959

Type Species

Furnishina furnishi Müller, 1959, *s.f.* from the Gallatin Limestone, Big Horn Mountains, Wyoming.

25

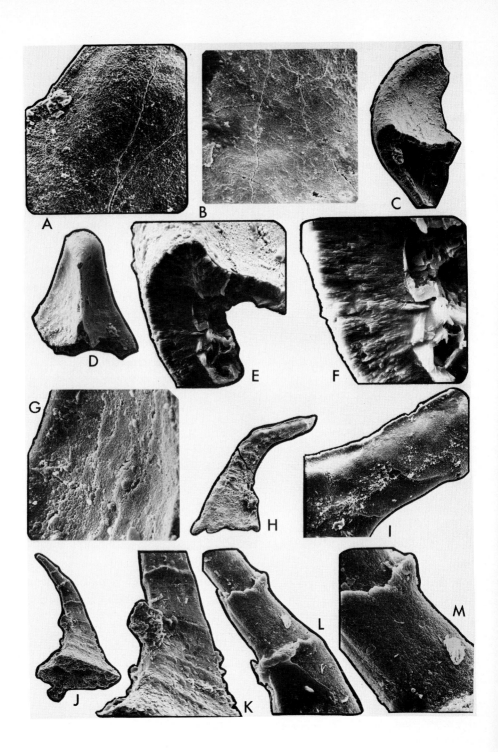

***Furnishina asymmetrica* Müller, 1959** *s.f.*

Figs. 7J–M

Furnishina asymmetrica Müller, 1959:451, 452, pl. 11, figs. 16a, b, 19.
Furnishina asymmetrica—Nogami, 1966:354, pl. 9, figs. 1a–2b.
Furnishina asymmetrica—Müller, 1971:8, pl. 1, figs. 13, 16.
Furnishina asymmetrica—Müller, 1973:39, pl. 1, figs. 6, 8, 9.
Furnishina asymmetrica—Lee, 1975:79, pl. 1, fig. 1, text-fig. 2A.
Furnishina asymmetrica—Miller and Paden, 1976:595, pl. 1, figs. 13, 14.
Furnishina asymmetrica—Abaimova, 1978:78, pl. 7, fig. 1.
Furnishina asymmetrica—Landing, 1979:22, pl. I–1, fig. 7.

Occurrence and Hypotype

One element (ROM 38374) from the *Cordylodus oklahomensis* Zone (KK 33). Trilobites of the *Apoplanias* Fauna and *Symphysurina brevispicata* Subzone were recovered, respectively, below (KK 43) and above (KK 25) sample KK 33.

Remarks

Furnishina asymmetrica s.f. and *F. furnishi* Müller are probably asymmetrical and subsymmetrical to symmetrical elements of the *F. furnishi* apparatus (Landing, 1979).

Paraconodont structure, or the aboral addition of growth lamellae which do not enclose the distal portion of the element (Bengtson, 1976), is shown by the detachment of the distal portion of growth lamellae from previously secreted portions of the sclerite (Figs. 7K–M).

Fig. 7A, B   *Fryxellodontus?* sp. nov., serrated element, ROM 38366, sample KK 146.
    A   Detail of posterolateral margin of cusp showing prismatic crystallites comprising posterior carina (compare Fig. 6L), ×269.
    B   Detail of lateral surface of cusp showing slightly corroded surface of originally smooth element (compare Fig. 6J), ×269.
  C-G   *Fryxellodontus inornatus* Miller, symmetrical element, ROM 38368, sample KK 43.
    C   Aboral-lateral view (note broken tip of element, compare Fig. 7D), ×215.
    D   Posterior view, ×151.
    E, F   Detail of crystallites oriented normal to wall of element (compare Fig. 7C), ×731 and ×1462, respectively.
    G   Detail of corroded outer surface of originally smooth element (compare Fig. 7D), ×153.
  H, I   Protoconodont sp. indet. *s.f.*, ROM 38375, sample KK* 135–150.
    H   Lateral view, ×47.
    I   Detail showing lower edges of basally-internally secreted lamellae, ×237.
  J-M   *Furnishina asymmetrica* Müller, *s.f.*, ROM 38374, sample KK 33.
    J   Posterior view, ×99.
    K-M   Detail of surface of element showing exfoliation of upper portions of paraconodont growth lamellae, ×290, ×247, ×989, respectively.

Genus *Oneotodus* Lindström, 1955

Type Species

Distacodus? simplex Furnish, 1938, *s.f.* from the Oneota Dolostone, Allamakee County, Iowa.

"Oneotodus" nakamurai Nogami, 1967
Fig. 8A–C

Oneotodus sp. A. Müller, 1959:458, pl. 13, fig. 17.

Oneotodus nakamurai Nogami, 1967:216, 217, pl. 1, figs. 9a–13, text-figs. 3A–E.

Oneotodus nakamurai—Miller, 1969:435, 436, pl. 63, figs. 1–9, text-fig. 5E (*pars,* pl. 63, fig. 10 = *"Acodus" sevierensis* Miller, 1969 *s.f.*).

Oneotodus simplex—Miller, 1970:101, 102, text-fig. 9D (*non O. simplex* Furnish, 1938, *s.f.*).

Oneotodus sp. aff. *simplex*—Miller, 1970:102, text-fig. 9E (*non O. simplex* [Furnish, 1938] *s.f.*).

Oneotodus datsonensis Druce and Jones, 1971:80, pl. 14, figs. 1a–3b, text-fig. 26c (*pars,* pl. 14, figs. 4a, b = *"Acodus" housensis* Miller, 1969, *s.f.*).

Oneotodus nakamurai—Druce and Jones, 1971:82, 83, pl. 10, figs. 3a–5c, 7a–8b, text-fig. 26i (*pars,* pl. 10, figs. 1, 2, 6a–c, text-fig. 26j = *Proconodontus notchpeakensis* Miller, 1969, *s.f.*).

Fig. 8A–C   *"Oneotodus" nakamurai* Nogami, ROM 38370, sample KK* 135–150.
- A   Lateral view of long-based element, ×95.
- B   Detail of subparallel striae (compare Fig. 8A), ×946.
- C   Detail of subparallel striae (centre of Fig. 8B), ×2365.
- D, E   *"Proconodontus" carinatus* Miller, scandodiform element, ROM 38362, sample KK 119.5.
  - D   Inner lateral view of aborally flaring side, ×129.
  - E   Corroded surface or originally smooth element, ×645.
- F   *"Proconodontus" carinatus* Miller, drepanodiform element, ROM 38365, sample KK 50, ×52.
- G, H   *"Proconodontus" carinatus* Miller, drepanodiform element, ROM 38369, sample KK 43.
  - G   Lateral view, ×108.
  - H   Detail of corroded surface of originally smooth element, ×538.
- I-L   *Proconodontus serratus* Miller *s.f.*, ROM 38363, sample KK 86.5.
  - I, J   Lateral views, ×52 and ×49, respectively.
  - K   Detail showing acicular crystallites composing denticulated oral edge (compare Fig. 8I), ×258.
  - L   Detail showing acicular crystallites comprising anterior carina (compare Fig. 8J), ×247.
- M, N   *"Prooneotodus" tenuis* (Müller), ROM 38364, sample KK 77.
  - M   Detail showing irregular lower (aboral) edges of basal, internally accreted, growth lamellae, ×58.
  - N   Anterior or posterior view of three-element incomplete half-apparatus (Landing, 1977). Third (lower) element largely obscured by upper two elements, ×581.
- O   *Phosphannulus universalis* Müller, Nogami, and Lenz, ROM 38361, sample KK 123. Oblique view of attachment surface, ×112.

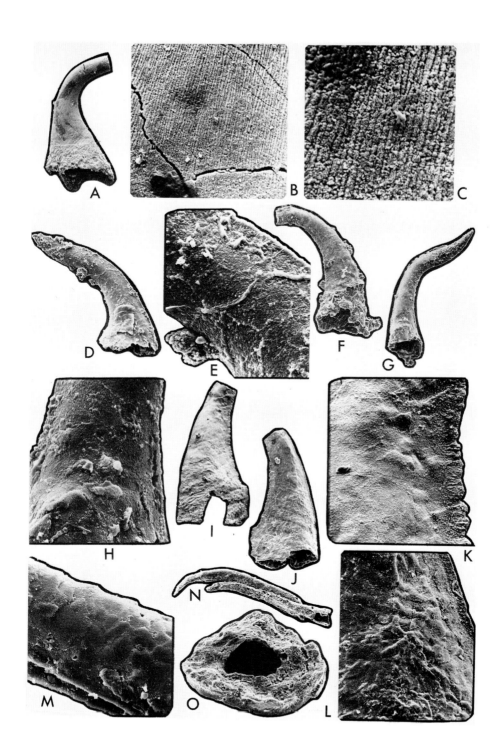

Oneotodus datsonensis—Jones, 1971:56, 57, pl. 3, figs. 5a–c, 7a–c.

Oneotodus nakamurai—Jones, 1971:58, pl. 4, figs. 1a–c, 3a–4c (*pars*, pl. 4, figs. 2a–c = *"Acontiodus" unicostatus* Miller, 1969, *s.f.*).

Oneotodus sp. aff. *simplex*—Miller and Melby, 1971:122, pl. 2, fig. 9 (*non O. simplex* [Furnish, 1938] *s.f.*).

Oneotodus nakamurai—Müller, 1971:10, text-fig. 1e.

Oneotodus nakamurai—Müller and Nogami, 1971:76, pl. 7, fig. 1, text-fig. 14B.

Oneotodus nakamurai—Müller, 1973:41, pl. 5, fig. 4.

Oneotodus nakamurai—Lee, 1975:81, pl. 1, figs. 6, 9, 10, text-figs. 2E, G.

Oneotodus nakamurai—Nowlan, 1976:294, 295, pl. 1, figs. 24–28.

Oneotodus nakamurai—Abaimova and Markov, 1977:92, 93, pl. 14, figs. 12–14, 16.

Oneotodus variabilis—Abaimova and Markov, 1977:93, pl. 14, fig. 11, pl. 15, fig. 4 (*non O. variabilis* Lindström, 1955, *s.f.*).

"Oneotodus" nakamurai—Landing, 1979:72, 73, 146, 147, 206, 207, pl. II–2, figs. 13–15, 17, pl. III–1, figs. 6, 7, pl. IV–1, figs. 8, 9.

Oneotodus simplex—Tipnis et al., 1979:31, pl. 1, fig. 18 (*non O. simplex* [Furnish, 1938] *s.f.*).

Oneotodus variabilis Lindström, Tipnis et al., 1979:31, pl. 1, figs. 20, 22.

Occurrence and Hypotype

Two elements from the *Bowmania americana* Fauna, samples KK* 135–150 (ROM 38370) and KK 78 (specimen lost).

Remarks

Miller (1969) restricted his concept of *Oneotodus nakamurai* to elements with a length:width ratio of the basal margin of 2:3 to 3:2. He assigned one of Nogami's figured specimens (Nogami, 1967: pl. 1, fig. 13) to *Semiacontiodus nogamii* Miller because of the strong anteroposterior flattening of the aboral margin of the element. Miller's (1969) taxonomic restriction stems from a failure to recover the species below the *Cordylodus oklahomensis* Zone. Landing (1979) noted that *"O."* *nakamurai* elements from the upper *Proconodontus* Zone in Vermont and New York tend to have longer bases than those from higher strata. In addition, *"O."* *nakamurai* elements with long bases from the *Proconodontus* Zone are often strongly aborally flattened or have a rounded triangular cross section of the aboral margin (Landing, 1979). The narrowly rounded anterolateral and oral margins of the illustrated specimen from the Rabbitkettle produce a triangular aboral cross section (Fig. 8A).

Discussion

"Oneotodus" nakamurai specimens are covered with fine, subparallel striations (Fig. 8B, C) and are consequently unique among conodont elements from *Proconodontus* and lower *Cordylodus oklahomensis* zones. The restriction of this surface microstructure to *"O." nakamurai* suggests that the apparatus is mono-elemental.

30

Although *"Oneotodus" nakamurai* elements may appear to be similar to *Proconodontus notchpeakensis* Miller *s.f.* (Miller, 1969:436), the latter are devoid of surface microsculpture (Landing, 1979; this report). *"Oneotodus" nakamurai* appears in uppermost Cambrian faunas without known ancestors. Long-based elements in the *Proconodontus* Zone are replaced by short-based forms in the *Cordylodus oklahomensis* Zone (Landing, 1979). These short-based elements were apparently ancestral to upper *C. oklahomensis* Zone forms such as Miller's (1969) *"Acodus" housensis s.f., "A." sevierensis s.f., Semiacontiodus*, and *"Paltodus" utahensis* Miller, 1969 *s.f.*, all of which are finely striated and albid (Landing, 1979).

Taxonomy

"Oneotodus" nakamurai elements are provisionally referred to *Oneotodus*. R. L. Ethington (pers. comm., 1979) notes that elements of the type species, *O. simplex*, have low lateral costae, a shallower basal cavity than that illustrated by Furnish (1938), and coarser striae than forms referred by other authors to *Oneotodus*. The basal cavity of *"O." nakamurai* extends to the point of maximum curvature of the finely striated element.

Genus *Proconodontus* Miller, 1969

Type Species

Proconodontus muelleri Miller, 1969, from the Notch Peak Limestone, House Range, west-central Utah.

"Proconodontus" carinatus Miller, 1969
Fig. 5C, F, 8D–H

Drepanodiform Element

Oneotodus sp. indet. Müller, 1959:458, pl. 13, fig. 15.
Proconodontus notchpeakensis Miller, 1969:458, pl. 66, figs. 21–29, text-fig. 5G.
Proconodontus notchpeakensis—Miller, 1970:105, 106, text-fig. 9M.
Oneotodus gallatini—Druce and Jones, 1971:81, 82, pl. 9, figs. 9a–c, pl. 10, figs. 9a–10c, text-figs. 26f, g (*non Proconodontus gallatini* [Müller, 1959] *s.f.*).
Proconodontus notchpeakensis—Müller, 1971:43, pl. 4, fig. 6.
Oneotodus nakamurai—Lee, 1975:81, (*pars*, pl. 1, fig. 9, *non "O." nakamurai* Nogami, 1966).
Proconodontus notchpeakensis—Nowlan, 1976:351, pl. 1, figs. 6, 7.
"Proconodontus" carinatus—Landing, 1979:78, 151, 152, 209, pl. II–3, fig. 12, pl. III–1, fig. 16, pl. IV–1, figs. 10, 11 (*pars*, cited figures are only of drepanodiform element).

Proconodontus notchpeakensis—Tipnis et al., 1979:31, pl. 1, fig. 14.
?Proconodontus cf. *P. notchpeakensis*—Tipnis et al., 1979:31, pl. 1, fig. 15.

Scandodiform Element

Proconodontus carinatus Miller, 1969:437, pl. 66, figs. 13–20, text-fig. 51.
Proconodontus carinatus—Miller, 1970:104, text-fig. 5I.
Proconodontus carinatus—Miller and Melby, 1971:122, pl. 2, figs. 16, 17.
Proconodontus aff. *carinatus*—Ozgül and Gedik, 1973:49, pl. 1, fig. 15.
Proconodontus carinatus—Nowlan, 1976:349, pl. 1, figs. 11, 12.
Proconodontus carinatus—Landing et al., 1978:76, fig. 2A.
Proconodontus carinatus—Landing, 1979:24, pl. I–1, fig. 8.
"Proconodontus" carinatus—Landing, 1979:78, 204, pl. II–3, fig. 9, pl. IV–1,
  fig. 14 (*pars*, cited figures are only of scandodiform element).

Occurrence

Thirteen scandodiform and 41 drepanodiform elements recovered in association with *Bowmania americana* Fauna through *Apoplanias* Fauna trilobites. A scandodiform element from KK* 0–12 occurs above the highest known trilobites (*Symphysurina brevispicata* Subzone) from KK 20.

Hypotypes

Scandodiform hypotype ROM 38362 from KK 119.5 and drepanodiform hypotypes ROM 38365 and 38369 from KK 50 and KK 43, respectively.

Remarks

Proconodontus carinatus s.f. and *P. notchpeakensis s.f.* have basal cavities which do not extend to the tip of the elements, and the cusps are albid above the basal cavity. The two form species differ from the completely hollow elements of *P. muelleri s.f.* and *P. serratus s.f.* although all four form species lack any surface microsculpture (Landing, 1979).

   Proconodontus carinatus s.f. and *P. notchpeakensis s.f.* regularly appear together at the base of the *P. notchpeakensis* Subzone (Miller, 1970; Derby et al., 1972) and persist into Fauna B (Miller, 1970, 1978). The two form species regularly occur together in continental slope deposits in the Appalachians (Landing, 1979). Similarity of range zones and regular association suggests that the two elements are part of a multi-element species (Miller, 1978; Landing, 1979). *Proconodontus notchpeakensis s.f.* and *P. carinatus s.f.* represent the bilaterally symmetrical (drepanodiform) and the aborally laterally flared (scandodiform) elements of the apparatus. These two elements are homologous, respectively, to the cordylodiform and cyrtoniodiform elements of bi-elemental *Cordylodus oklahomensis*. A further similarity between these two apparatuses is that the bilaterally symmetrical to subsymmetrical drepanodiform and cordylodiform elements are numerically dominant. However it is possible that the element ratio differs between the two species. Miller (1978) recovered the elements in a drepanodiform:scandodiform ratio of 3837:1471 (1:0.38) at the Lava Dam Five section in the Notch Peak Limestone, Utah. The ratio in the sparse Rabbitkettle collection is 41:13 (1:0.32). These data suggest that scandodiform elements were proportionately better represented in *"Proconodontus"* carinatus than the corresponding cyrtoniodiform elements in *Cordylodus oklahomensis*.

"Proconodontus" carinatus is here provisionally referred to *Proconodontus*. The elements of this bi-elemental apparatus differ strongly from the type species *Proconodontus muelleri s.f.* In addition, the *P. muelleri* apparatus appears to have been mono-elemental (Landing, 1979).

Proconodontus serratus Miller, 1969, *s.f.*
Fig. 8I–L

Proconodontus mülleri serratus Miller, 1969:438, pl. 66, figs. 41–44.
Proconodontus muelleri serratus—Miller, 1969:105, text-fig. 9L.
Coelocerodontus burkei Druce and Jones, 1971:61, 62, pl. 11, figs. 5a–6c, 8a–c, text-fig. 22e (*pars,* pl. 11, figs. 7a–c, 9–12b, text-fig. 22a = *Proconodontus muelleri* Miller, 1969, *s.f.*).
Proconodontus serratus—Müller, 1973:44, pl. 4, figs. 1a-2.
Proconodontus serratus—Landing, 1979:79, 80, 153, 210, 211, pl. II-3, fig. 16, pl. III-1, fig. 4, pl. IV-1, figs. 12, 15.

Occurrence and Hypotype

Recovered from the *Bowmania americana* Fauna, sample KK 86.5 (two elements) and KK* 135–150 (one element). Hypotype ROM 38363 from KK 86.5.

Remarks

Proconodontus muelleri Miller, *s.f.* and *P. serratus s.f.* have basal cavities reaching almost to the tip of the elements, differ in the serrated posterior edge of the latter (Miller, 1969), and lack surface microsculpture (Landing, 1979). The posterior edge of *P. serratus s.f.* may be almost completely serrated (Fig. 8I, J) or may have only a few denticles near the aboral margin or distally (Landing, 1979). The co-occurrence of *P. muelleri s.f.* and *P. serratus* in the upper *Saukia* Zone (Miller, 1969-1978; Landing, 1979) may mean that one conodont animal bore both types of elements. The absence of *P. serratus s.f.* in the lower *Saukia* Zone (Miller, 1975, 1977) possibly means that denticulation has not appeared in some of the elements of an essentially mono-elemental *P. muelleri* apparatus.

Dissolution of the surface of the elements from Section KK reveals that the anterior carina (Fig. 8L) and posterior serrated edge (Fig. 8K) are comprised of acicular crystallites oriented parallel to the plane of lateral flattening of the elements.

33

Genus *Prooneotodus* Müller and Nogami, 1971

Type Species

Oneotodus gallatini Müller, 1959, *s.f.* from the Gallatin Limestone, Big Horn Mountains, Wyoming.

"Prooneotodus" tenuis (Müller, 1959)
Fig. 8M, N

Oneotodus tenuis Müller, 1959:457, 458, pl. 13, figs. 11, 13, 14, 20.
Oneotodus tenuis—Nogami, 1966:356, pl. 9, figs. 11, 12.
Oneotodus tenuis—Clark and Robison, 1969:1045, text-fig. 1a.
Oneotodus tenuis—Miller, 1969:436, pl. 64, figs. 43–45, text-fig. 5C.
Oneotodus tenuis—Müller, 1971:8, pl. 1, figs. 1a, v, 4–6.
Prooneotodus tenuis—Müller, 1973:45, pl. 1, figs. 1-36.
Oneotodus tenuis—Ozgül and Gedik, 1973:48, pl. 1, figs. 2, 10, 12.
Prooneotodus tenuis—Lee, 1975:83, 84, pl. 1, figs. 14–17, text-figs. 2K, L.
Prooneotodus tenuis—Miller and Paden, 1976:596, pl. 1, figs. 20–23.
Prooneotodus tenuis—Müller and Andres, 1976:193–200, pl. 22, figs. A, B, text-figs. 1a–3.
"Prooneotodus" tenuis—Landing, 1977:1072–1084, pl. 1, fig. 1–9, pl. 2, figs. 1–11, text-fig. 1
"Prooneotodus" tenuis—Landing et al., 1978:76, text-fig. 2B.
Prooneotodus tenuis—Abaimova, 1978:83, pl. 8, figs. 2, 4, 9.
Prooneotodus savitskyi Abaimova, 1978:82, 83, pl. 7, figs. 13, 14, pl. 8, fig. 1.
"Prooneotodus" tenuis—Landing, 1979:25, 82, 83, 153, 154, 212, 225–250, pl. I–1, fig. 12, pl. II–3, fig. 18, pl. III–1, fig. 3, pl. IV–1, fig. 3, pl. V–1, figs. 1–9, pl. V–2, figs. 1–11, text-fig. V–1.
Oneotodus tenuis—Tipnis et al., 1979:31, pl. 1, fig. 6.

Occurrence and Hypotype

Two elements from the *Missisquoia depressa* Subzone, samples KK 50 and KK 116, and the hypotype (ROM 38364) three element incomplete half-apparatus (Landing, 1977) from the *Bowmania americana* Fauna, sample KK 77.

Remarks

The elements of *"Prooneotodus" tenuis* have protoconodont structure and the species cannot be brought to the paraconodont genus *Prooneotodus* (Landing, 1977).

Dissolution of the exterior surface of the elements from Section KK has apparently obscured the fine longitudinal striations present in elements of the species (Müller, 1971; Landing, 1977) and caused irregular exfoliation of the growth lamellae (Fig. 8M).

34

Protoconodont sp. indet. *s.f.*
Fig. 5G, 7H, I

?Furnishina? sp. Tipnis et al., 1979:31, pl. 1, fig. 5.

Occurrence and Hypotype

Two specimens (hypotype ROM 38375) from the *Bowmania americana* Fauna (KK* 135–150).

Description

The form is known from gently curved, asymmetrical, conelike, proclined elements with sharp posterior costa. The anterior costa becomes rounded aborally and a rounded anterolateral costa is present. The internal cavity extends nearly to the end of the thin-walled elements.

Remarks

The specimens have a superficial resemblance to the euconodont *Proconodontus muelleri* Miller *s.f.* and to the paraconodont *Furnishina primitiva* Müller *s.f.* However, examination of the surface of the elements (Fig. 5I) shows that they grew by basal-internal addition of growth lamellae and have protoconodont structure (Bengtson, 1976).

Tipnis et al. (1979) illustrated a similar element from section K (sample K 525).

Order Hyolithelminthes Fisher, 1962
Family Phosphannulidae Müller, Nogami, and Lenz, 1974
Genus *Phosphannulus* Müller, Nogami, and Lenz, 1974

Type Species

Phosphannulus universalis Müller, Nogami, and Lenz from the Upper Silurian Beyrichien-Kalke, Berlin Spandau-West.

Phosphannulus universalis Müller, Nogami, and Lenz, 1974
Fig. 8O

Form B Webers, 1966:72, pl. 14, figs. 3, 6.
Phosphannulus universalis Müller, Nogami, and Lenz, 1974:91, 92, pl. 18, figs. 1–12, pl. 19, figs. 1–13, pl. 20, figs. 1–7, pl. 21, figs. 1–9, text-figs. 1–6.
Phosphannulus sp. Winder, 1976:654, pl. 2, fig. 11.
Phosphannulus universalis—Landing, 1979:28, 215, pl. I–1, fig. 2, pl. IV–1, fig. 7.

35

Occurrence and Hypotype

Recovered from the *Yukonaspis kindlei* Fauna through *Missisquoia* sp. nov. Fauna. Four specimens from KK 33 occur in an interval lying below the *Symphysurina brevispicata* Subzone and above the *Apoplanias* Fauna. Hypotype ROM 38361 from the *Missisquoia* sp. nov. Fauna (KK 123).

Remarks

The form, an attachment structure secreted by a possible hyolithelminthoid epizoan (Müller et al., 1974), ranges from the Late Cambrian through Late Devonian. It has been reported from North America, Iran, and Baltoscandia.

Acknowledgements

Landing studied the conodont faunas of this report as a post-doctoral fellow at the University of Waterloo with Dr. C. R. Barnes as supervisor. Ludvigsen's field work was supported by a grant from the Natural Sciences and Engineering Research Council. Mr. Peter Fenton, University of Toronto, ably assisted in the field. Dr. C. R. Barnes reviewed the preliminary manuscript. The electron microscopy was done by Mr. George Gomolka, Department of Geology, University of Toronto.

We are grateful to all of the individuals mentioned above. We also thank the two reviewers whose critical comments improved the paper.

Literature Cited

ABAIMOVA, G.P.
　1975　Early Ordovician conodonts from the middle reaches of the Lena River.　Transaction Series of the Siberian Scientific Research Institute for Geology, Geophysics and Mineralogy, Novosibirsk, 207:1–129. [In Russian].
　1978　First Cambrian conodonts from the central region of Kazakhstan.　Paleontological Journal 17:77–87. [In Russian].

ABAIMOVA, G.P. and Ye. P. MARKOV
　1977　First recovery of conodonts of the lowest Ordovician *Cordylodus proavus* Zone on the southern Siberian Platform. *In* Sokolov, V.S. and A.V. Kanygin, eds., Stratigraphic problems of the Ordovician and Silurian of Siberia.　Transactions of the Institute of Geology and Geophysics, Academy of Sciences SSSR, Siberian Section, Novosibirsk, 372:86–94. [In Russian].

BARNES, C.R. and M.L.S. POPLAWSKI
　1973　Lower and Middle Ordovician conodonts from the Mystic Formation, Quebec, Canada.　Journal of Paleontology 47:760–790.

BARNES, C.R., C.B. REXROAD, and J.F. MILLER
　1973　Lower Paleozoic conodont provincialism. *In* Rhodes, F.H.T., ed., Conodont paleozoology.　Geological Society of America, Special Paper 141:157–190.

BENGTSON, S.
　1976　The structure of some Middle Cambrian conodonts, and the early evolution of conodont structure and function.　Lethaia 9:185–206.

BERGSTRÖM, S.M. and W.C. SWEET
　1966　Conodonts from the Lexington Limestone (Middle Ordovician) of Kentucky and its lateral equivalents in Ohio and Indiana.　Bulletins of American Paleontology 50:271–441.

CECILE, M.P.
　1978　Report on Road River stratigraphy and the Misty Creek Embayment, Bonnet Plume (106B), and surrounding map-areas, Northwest Territories.　Geological Survey of Canada, Paper 78–1A:371–377.

CLARK, D.L. and R.A. ROBISON
　1969　Oldest conodonts in North America.　Journal of Paleontology 40:1044–1046.

COOK, H.E.
　1972　Miette platform evolution and relation to overlying bank (''reef'') localization, Upper Devonian, Alberta.　Bulletin of Canadian Petroleum Geology 20:375–411.

DERBY, J.R., H.R. LANE, and B.S. NORFORD
　1972　Uppermost Cambrian—basal Ordovician faunal succession in Alberta and correlation with similar sequences in the western United States.　24th International Geological Congress, Montreal, 1972, Proceedings 7:503–512.

DRUCE, E.C.
　1978　Correlation of the Cambrian/Ordovician boundary in Australia. *In* Belford, B.J. and V. Scheibnerova, eds., The Crespin volume: essays in honour of Irene Crespin.　Australia Bureau of Mineral Resources, Geology and Geophysics, Bulletin 192:49–60.

DRUCE, E.C. and P.J. JONES
　1971　Cambro-Ordovician conodonts from the Burke River structural belt, Queensland.　Australia Bureau of Mineral Resources, Geology and Geophysics, Bulletin 110:1–167.

EICHENBERG, W.
　1930　Conodonten aus dem Culm des Harzes.　Paläontologische Zeitschrift 12:177–182.

EPSTEIN, A.G., J.B. EPSTEIN, and L.D. HARRIS

1977   Conodont color alteration—an index to organic metamorphism.   United States Geological
        Survey Professional Paper 995:1–27.

ETHINGTON, R.L. and D.L. CLARK

1971   Lower Ordovician conodonts of North America. *In* Sweet, W.C. and S.M. Bergström, eds.,
        Symposium on conodont biostratigraphy. Geological Society of America, Memoir
        127:21–61.

FÅHRAEUS, L.E. and G.S. NOWLAN

1978   Franconian (Late Cambrian) to Early Champlainian (Middle Ordovician) conodonts from the
        Cow Head Group, western Newfoundland.   Journal of Paleontology 52:444–471.

FISHER, D.W.

1962   Small conoidal shells of uncertain affinities. *In* Moore, R.C., ed., Treatise on Invertebrate
        Paleontology, Part W, Miscellanea.   Lawrence, Geological Society of America and Univer-
        sity of Kansas Press, pp. W98–W143.

FORTEY, R.A.

1975   Early Ordovician trilobite communities. *In* Martinsson, A., ed., Evolution and morphology of
        the Trilobita, Trilobitoidea and Merostomata.   Fossils and Strata 4:331–352.

FURNISH, W.M.

1938   Conodonts from the Prairie du Chien (Lower Ordovician) beds of the Upper Mississippi Val-
        ley.   Journal of Paleontology 12:318–340.

GABRIELSE, H.

1967   Tectonic evolution of the northern Canadian Cordillera.   Canadian Journal of Earth Sciences
        4:271–298.

GABRIELSE, H., S.L. BUSSON, and J.A. RODDICK

1973   Geology of the Flat River, Glacier Lake, and Wrigley Lake Map-Areas, District of Mackenzie
        and Yukon Territory.   Geological Survey of Canada, Memoir 366:1–153.

JONES, P.J.

1971   Lower Ordovician conodonts from the Bonaparte Gulf Basin and the Daly River Basin, north-
        western Australia.   Australia Bureau of Mineral Resources, Geology and Geophysics, Bulle-
        tin 117:1–80.

JONES, P.J., J.H. SHERGOLD, and E.C. DRUCE

1971   Late Cambrian and Early Ordovician stages in western Queensland.   Journal of the Geologi-
        cal Society of Australia 18:1–32.

KURTZ, V.E.

1976   Biostratigraphy of the Cambrian and lowest Ordovician, Bighorn Mountains and associated
        uplifts in Wyoming and Montana. *In* Robison, R.A. and A.J. Rowell, eds., Paleontology and
        depositional environments: Cambrian of western North America.   Brigham Young Univer-
        sity, Geological Studies 23:215–227.

LANDING, E.

1977   *"Prooneotodus" tenuis* (Müller, 1959) apparatuses from the Taconic allochthon, eastern New
        York: construction, taphonomy, and the protoconodont "supertooth" model.   Journal of Pa-
        leontology 51:1072–1084.

1978   Conodonts from the Gorge Formation (Late Cambrian—(now) Early Ordovician), north-
        western Vermont.   Geological Society of America, Abstracts with Programs 10:219. [Ab-
        stract].

1979   Studies in Late Cambrian–Early Ordovician conodont biostratigraphy and paleoecology,
        northern Appalachian region.   Ph.D. Thesis, University of Michigan. 308 pp.

LANDING. E., M.E. TAYLOR, and B.-D. ERDTMANN

 1978   Correlation of the Cambrian-Ordovician boundary between the Acado-Baltic and North American faunal provinces.   Geology 6:75–78.

LEE. H.-Y.

 1975   Conodonts from the Upper Cambrian formations, Kangweon-Do, South Korea and its stratigraphical significance.   Yonsei University, Graduate School Bulletin 12:71–89.

LINDSTRÖM. M.

 1955   Conodonts from the lowermost Ordovician strata of south-central Sweden.   Geologiska Föreningen i Stockholm, Förhandlingar 76:517 – 6 03.

LOCHMAN-BALK. C. and J.L. WILSON

 1958   Cambrian biostratigraphy in North America.   Journal of Paleontology 32:312–350.

LONGACRE. S.A.

 1970   Trilobites of the Upper Cambrian Ptychaspid Biomere, Wilberns Formation, Central Texas.   Paleontological Society Memoir 4:1–70.

LUDVIGSEN. R.

 1975   Ordovician formations and faunas, southern Mackenzie Mountains.   Canadian Journal of Earth Sciences 12:663–697.

 1979a Middle Ordovician trilobite biofacies, southern Mackenzie Mountains. *In* Stelck, C.R. and B.D.E. Chatterton, eds., Western and Arctic Canadian biostratigraphy.   Geological Association of Canada, Special Paper 18:1–37.

 1979b Trilobite biostratigraphy of the Cambrian-Ordovician boundary beds of the Rabbitkettle Formation, western District of Mackenzie.   Canadian Biostratigraphy and Paleontology Seminar, Edmonton, September, 1979. [Abstract].

MILLER, J.F.

 1969   Conodont faunas of the Notch Peak Limestone (Cambro-Ordovician), House Range, Utah.   Journal of Paleontology 43:413–439.

 1970   Conodont evolution and biostratigraphy of the Upper Cambrian and lowest Ordovician.   Ph.D. Thesis, University of Wisconsin. 137 pp.

 1975   Conodont faunas from the Cambrian and lowest Ordovician of western North America.   Geological Society of America, Abstracts with Programs 7:1200–1201. [Abstract].

 1977   Conodont biostratigraphy and intercontinental correlations across the Cambrian-Ordovician boundary.   25th International Geological Congress, Sydney, 1977, Proceedings 1:274.

 1978   Upper Cambrian and lowest Ordovician conodont faunas of the House Range, Utah. *In* Miller, J.F., ed., Upper Cambrian to Middle Ordovician conodont faunas of western Utah.   Southwest Missouri State University, Geosciences Series 5:1–33.

MILLER. J.F. and H.J. MELBY

 1971   Trempealeauan conodonts. *In* Clark, D.L., ed., Conodonts and biostratigraphy of the Wisconsin Paleozoic.   Wisconsin Geological and Natural History Survey, Information Circular 19:4–9, 78–81.

MILLER. R.H. and E.A. PADEN

 1976   Upper Cambrian stratigraphy and conodonts from eastern California.   Journal of Paleontology 50:590–597.

MÜLLER. K.J.

 1959   Kambrische Conodonten.   Zeitschrift der Deutschen Geologischen Gesellschaft 111:431–485.

 1971   Cambrian conodont faunas. *In* Sweet, W.C. and S.M. Bergström, eds., Symposium on conodont biostratigraphy.   Geological Society of America, Memoir 127:5–20.

 1973   Late Cambrian and Early Ordovician conodonts from northern Iran.   Geological Survey of Iran, Report 3:1–76.

MÜLLER, K.J. and D. ANDRES

    1976   Eine Conodontengruppe von *Prooneotodus tenuis* (Müller, 1959) in natürlichem Zusammenhang aus dem oberen Kambrium von Schweden.   Paläontologische Zeitschrift 50:193–200.

MÜLLER, K.J. and Y. NOGAMI

    1971   Über den Feinbau der Conodonten.   Kyoto University, Memoirs of the Faculty of Science, Series of Geology and Mineralogy 38:1–87.

MÜLLER, K.J., Y. NOGAMI, and H. LENZ

    1974   Phosphatische Ringe als Mikrofossilien im Altpaläozoikum.   Palaeontographica (Abt. A) 146:79–99.

NOGAMI, Y.

    1966   Kambrische Conodonten von China, Teil 1.   Kyoto University, College of Sciences Memoir 33:211–218.

NORFORD, B.S. and R.W. MACQUEEN

    1975   Lower Paleozoic Franklin Mountain and Mount Kindle Formations, District of Mackenzie: their type sections and regional development.   Geological Survey of Canada, Paper 74–34:1–37.

NOWLAN, G.S.

    1976   Late Cambrian to Late Ordovician conodont evolution and biostratigraphy of the Franklinian Miogeosyncline, eastern Canadian Arctic Islands.   Ph.D. Thesis, University of Waterloo. 591 pp.

ÖZGÜL, N. and I. GEDIK

    1973   Caltepe Limestone of Lower Paleozoic age from the middle Taurus Mountains and new information about the stratigraphy and conodonts of the Seydesehir Formation.   Turkish Geological Association Bulletin 16:39–52. [In Turkish].

PANDER, C.H.

    1856   Monographie der fossilen Fische des silurischen Systems der russisch-baltischen Gouvernements.   St. Petersburg, Buchdruckerei der Kaiserlichen Akademie der Wissenschaften. 91 pp.

REINHARDT, J.

    1974   Stratigraphy, sedimentology and Cambro-Ordovician paleogeography of the Frederick Valley, Maryland.   Maryland Geological Survey, Report of Investigation 23:1–73.

REPETSKI, J.E.

    1975   Conodonts from the El Paso Group (Lower Ordovician) of west Texas.   Ph.D. Thesis, University of Missouri. 239 pp.

ROEHL, P.O.

    1967   Stony Mountain (Ordovician) and Interlake (Silurian) facies analogs of recent low-energy marine and subaerial carbonates, Bahamas. American Association of Petroleum Geologists Bulletin 51:1971–2031.

ROSS, R.J., Jr.

    1975   Early Paleozoic trilobites, sedimentary facies, lithospheric plates, and ocean currents. *In* Martinsson, A., ed., Evolution and morphology of the Trilobita, Trilobitoidea and Merostomata.   Fossils and Strata 4:307–329.

SHINN, E.A.

    1968   Practical significance of birdseye structures in carbonate rocks.   Journal of Sedimentary Petrology 38:215–223.

41

STITT, J.H.

    1971   Cambrian-Ordovician trilobites, western Arbuckle Mountains. Oklahoma Geological Survey Bulletin 110:1–83.

    1977   Late Cambrian and earliest Ordovician trilobites, Wichita Mountains area, Oklahoma. Oklahoma Geological Survey Bulletin 124:1–79.

SWEET, W.C. and S.M. BERGSTRÖM

    1972   Multielement taxonomy and Ordovician conodonts. Geologica et Palaeontologica, Sonderband 1:29–42.

TAYLOR, M.E.

    1977   Late Cambrian of western North America: trilobite biofacies, environmental significance, and biostratigraphic implications. *In* Kauffman, E.G. and J.E. Hazel, eds., Concepts and methods of biostratigraphy. Stroudsburg, Dowden, Hutchinson and Ross, pp. 397–425.

TIPNIS, R.S., B.D.E. CHATTERTON, and R. LUDVIGSEN

    1979   Ordovician conodont biostratigraphy of the southern District of Mackenzie, Canada. *In* Stelck, C.R. and B.D.E. Chatterton, eds., Western and Arctic Canadian biostratigraphy. Geological Association of Canada, Special Paper 18:39–91.

VIIRA, V.

    1974   Ordovician conodonts of the Baltic. Tallin, Institute of Geology of the Estonian SSR Scientific Academy. 142 pp. [In Russian].

WAMEL, W.A. van

    1974   Conodont biostratigraphy of the Upper Cambrian and Lower Ordovician of north-western Öland, south-eastern Sweden. Utrecht Micropaleontology Bulletin 10:1–126.

WEBERS, G.F.

    1966   The Middle and Upper Ordovician conodont faunas of Minnesota. Minnesota Geological Survey Special Publication 4:1–123.

WILSON, J.L.

    1969   Microfacies and sedimentary structures in "deeper water" lime mudstone. *In* Friedman, G.M., ed., Depositional environments in carbonate rocks. Society of Economic Paleontologists and Mineralogists Special Publication 14:4–19.

    1970   Depositional facies across carbonate shelf margins. Transactions of the Gulf Coast Association Geological Society 20:229–233.

    1974   Characteristics of carbonate platform margins. American Association of Petroleum Geologists Bulletin 58:810–824.

WINDER, C.G.

    1976   Enigmatic objects in North American Ordovician carbonates. *In* Bassett, M.G., ed., The Ordovician System: Proceedings of a Palaeontological Association Symposium, Birmingham. Cardiff, University of Wales Press and National Museum of Wales, pp. 645–657.

WINSTON, D. and H. NICHOLLS

    1967   Late Cambrian and Early Ordovician faunas from the Wilberns Formation of Central Texas. Journal of Paleontology 41:66–96.